D1484688

The Kindergarten Survival Handbook

The Before School Checklist
&
A Guide for Parents

Allana Cummings Elovson, Ph. D.

Illustrations by Andrea Karin Elovson

ACKNOWLEDGMENTS

The author wishes to express her profound and enduring gratitude first to the families of California's Project Home Start, whose devotion to their children and hunger for knowledge to help them enhance their lives provided the inspiration for this book. Acknowledgement is also given for the help and encouragement of Dr. Anne O'Keefe, former National Home Start Director and the staff of Home Visitors of California's Home Start Program; to Dr. Kerby Alvy of the Center for the Improvement of Child Caring in Los Angeles, to Eleanor Franquez of L.A. County Head Start; to Sherrill Britten, Pat Boerger, Donald Kennedy, and to the generous and selfless help of kindergarten teachers Barbara Erdman, Yuri Hayashi, Constance Lint, Helen Hyun–Jou Park, Anne Pavlek, Jane Sierra, Barbara Sparks, Diane Tichy, Carol Waco, and Gail Yanai of the Los Angeles Unified School System; to Mary-Ellen Cassman, Jill Atkinson and Dr. Sharon Merritt, who egged me on; to Joy Cha and Marty Frame, staunch and patient companions of the revision, and above all, to Penny Paine and my family; John, John Harald, and Andrea, without whose unwavering support and immense and multifaceted efforts, both personal and graphic, this book would never have been possible.

Parent Education Resources
752 18th Street
Santa Monica, CA 90402

Cover design and illustrations: Andrea Karin Elovson

Copyright **1993** Allana Cummings Elovson

Sixteenth Printing, 2007

Publisher's Cataloging in Publication Data

Elovson, Allana Cummings

The Kindergarten Survival Handbook
The Before School Checklist and A Guide for Parents

Library of Congress Catalog Card Number 91-061432

1. Parent participation 2. Education: preschool 3. Child-rearing

ISBN 1-879888-06-8

All rights reserved except for the inclusion of brief quotations in a review. No part of this book may be reproduced or used in any form or by any means, electronic or mechanical, inclusing photocoying, recording, or by any information storage and retrieval system, without permission in writing from the author.

The information contained in this book is true, complete and accurate to the best of our knowledge. All recommendations and suggestions are made without any guarantees on the part of the author or publisher. The author and publisher disclaim all liability incurred in connection with the use of this information.

Design: Penelope C. Paine

A Letter To Parents

Dear Parents,

Going to school for the first time is one of the most important experiences in a child's life. School can be an exciting place, where children meet new and different people and get to do many new and different things. There's a lot to see, a lot to do, and a lot to learn.

If children are ready for kindergarten, it can be a wonderful experience that makes them feel good about themselves, good about school, and eager to learn.

But if children aren't ready, beginning school can be confusing and embarrassing, even frightening. Both boys and girls can start to feel bad about themselves, to dislike school, and not do as well as they could. This can happen if a child hasn't been to any school before, is new to the neighborhood or the country, or speaks a different language from most of the other children. Once a child feels this way, it can be very hard to change.

Many children also go to school unprepared because their parents, or others who care for them, are not aware of what children need to know to be ready for school, and that they, themselves are the best people to teach these to them. But it doesn't have to be this way. This book was written to help parents understand what children need to know, and to help them become children's best, as well as their first and most important, teachers.

The best way to use this book is to sit down, without your child around, and go through each section of THE BEFORE SCHOOL CHECKLIST. It helps to do this with someone else who knows your child, too. The Checklist is in eight sections, each about different kinds of things children need to know. If your child has already learned most of these, he or she is probably ready to start school and get a lot out of it. But if there are quite a few things your child hasn't yet learned, or some particular kinds of things your child doesn't yet do, you are the best person to teach these. The next part of this book, A GUIDE FOR PARENTS will show you how.

The GUIDE is also in eight sections. Each shows simple things you can do, at home or anywhere, to teach children the kinds of things they need to know. You won't need any special equipment or expensive toys. You won't even need any extra time. I know, because I've done all of these with my own children. Children can learn everything they need to know, and learn it best, from sharing simple everyday experiences with you. There's also some advice on how to teach things to children in ways that make it fun for both of you. Be patient, and encouraging, and the two of you will become good friends, and understand each other better, doing these enjoyable things together.

Remember, when children start school, they still need your help, but in other ways, as well. They'll need to know that you really care about what happens at school, and that you want to help. The last part of this book can help you take THE NEXT STEP into school, right along with them. Remember, you will always be the most important person in your children's education.

Best wishes,

Allana Elovson, Ph. D.

The Kindergarten Survival Handbook

A Letter to Parents

THE BEFORE SCHOOL CHECKLIST

A GUIDE FOR PARENTS

THE NEXT STEP

Before children start school, there are some things they need to know so they will understand what's going on around them, and what teachers and other people are talking about.

There are also things they need to know so they can learn the new things they'll be taught in school. Some don't seem to have much to do with school, but they are important.

1. Things They Need to Know

Before children start school, it would help if they could

1. KNOW THEIR OWN

	YES	NOT YET
name (first and last)	——	——
age	——	——
sex	——	——
phone number	——	——
address, or street of home.	——	——

2. KNOW THE NAMES AND RELATIONS OF FAMILY MEMBERS.

	YES	NOT YET
mother ("Mommy, her name is Anna.")	——	——
father (Joe)	——	——
brother (Joey)	——	——
sister ("Maria, she's my sister.")	——	——
grandparents	——	——

3. NAME SEVERAL PARTS OF THEIR OWN BODY.

	YES	NOT YET
head	——	——
face	——	——
hair	——	——
eyes	——	——
nose	——	——
mouth	——	——
ears	——	——
chin	——	——

Before children start school, it would help if they could

4. **POINT TO THEIR OWN**

	YES	NOT YET
neck	____	____
cheek	____	____
arms	____	____
hands	____	____
fingers	____	____
stomach	____	____

	YES	NOT YET
back	____	____
legs	____	____
knees	____	____
feet	____	____
toes	____	____

5. **KNOW THE NAMES OF THEIR CLOTHES.**

	YES	NOT YET
pants	____	____
socks, shoes	____	____
sweater	____	____
coat, jacket	____	____
shirt, blouse	____	____

1. Things They Need to Know

Before children start school, it would help if they could

6. NAME SOME THINGS AROUND THE HOUSE.

	YES	NOT YET
couch	___	___
bed	___	___
door	___	___
steps	___	___
stove	___	___
sink	___	___
pots	___	___
pans	___	___
broom	___	___

	YES	NOT YET
mop	___	___
window	___	___
shelf	___	___
closet	___	___
table	___	___
chair	___	___
garbage can	___	___
refrigerator	___	___

7. NAME SOME COMMON ANIMALS.

	YES	NOT YET
cat	___	___
horse	___	___
dog	___	___
birds	___	___
cow	___	___

maybe some zoo animals, too.

Before children start school, it would help if they could

8.   KNOW THE NAMES OF SOME FOODS.

	YES	NOT YET
milk	____	____
bread	____	____
fruit	____	____
vegetables	____	____
beans	____	____
meat	____	____
cheese	____	____
eggs	____	____

9.   KNOW SOME WORDS FOR HOW THINGS FEEL.

	YES	NOT YET
hard	____	____
soft	____	____
smooth	____	____
wet	____	____
dry	____	____
sharp	____	____
heavy	____	____
slippery	____	____
light	____	____
rough	____	____

1. Things They Need to Know

Before children start school, it would help if they could

10. KNOW SOME WORDS FOR WHEN THINGS HAPPEN.

YES   NOT YET

now   ——   ——

later   ——   ——

soon   ——   ——

never   ——   ——

always   ——   ——

sometimes   ——   ——

at night   ——   ——

in the daytime   ——   ——

11. KNOW THAT MONEY BUYS THINGS.

YES   NOT YET

——   ——

12. RECOGNIZE COINS FROM OTHER THINGS.

YES   NOT YET

——   ——

10

Before children start school, it would help if they could

13. KNOW SOME WORDS FOR WHERE THINGS ARE.

	YES	NOT YET
first	____	____
last	____	____
bottom	____	____
top	____	____

	YES	NOT YET
in	____	____
out	____	____
over	____	____
under	____	____
on	____	____
off	____	____
up	____	____
down	____	____
high	____	____
low	____	____

14. KNOW SOME WORDS FOR HOW THINGS LOOK.

	YES	NOT YET
fat	____	____
skinny	____	____
short	____	____
tall	____	____
small	____	____
big	____	____
little	____	____

1. Things They Need to Know

Before children start school, it would help if they could

15. KNOW SOME WORDS FOR HOW THINGS MOVE (or don't).

	YES	NOT YET
stop	——	——
go	——	——
come	——	——
away	——	——
fast	——	——
slowly	——	——
quickly	——	——

16. KNOW SOMETHING ABOUT THE PLACES AROUND THEM AND WHAT HAPPENS AT THEM.

	YES	NOT YET		YES	NOT YET
stores	——	——	gas station	——	——
school	——	——	fire station	——	——
hospital	——	——	doctor's office	——	——
church	——	——	dentist's office	——	——

Before children start school, it would help if they could

17. **TELL WHICH OF TWO THINGS IS BIGGER OR SMALLER.**

YES   NOT YET

____   ____

18. **POINT TO THE LARGEST OF 3 DIFFERENT THINGS.**

YES   NOT YET

____   ____

19. **COUNT 1, 2, 3, 4, 5 THINGS.**

YES   NOT YET

____   ____

20. **UNDERSTAND WORDS FOR HOW THINGS COMPARE.**

YES   NOT YET

	YES	NOT YET
same	____	____
different	____	____
more	____	____
less	____	____
all	____	____
none	____	____
taller	____	____
shorter	____	____
empty	____	____
full	____	____

For some ways parents can help their children learn the things they need to know, please see A Guide for Parents, pages 49-56.

These first pages, *"Things They Need to Know,"* showed many of the general things about the world around them that really help children feel comfortable when they enter kindergarten, and be ready and eager to learn. The next pages deal with some of the more specific things that children need to be able to do before they go to kindergarten.

While speaking clearly, using their hands well, and doing things for themselves may not seem to have much to do with school work, they are the building blocks for what they'll be taught in school. Knowing these things *before* kindergarten makes it easier for children to learn and for their teachers to teach them.

An important part of children's being ready for school is to be able to understand when teachers and other people speak to them. Even in kindergarten, there are many instructions and many questions and answers. If children don't understand the teacher, they won't be able to learn and they won't know what to do.

It's also very important that teachers and others can understand them, too. If they can't be understood by others, they won't be able to tell people what they want, or show they understand, and a lot of things could go wrong. Other children might make fun of them too, and your child might become unhappy about going to school or being with new people.

2. Understanding and Being Understood

Before children start school, it would help if they could

21. **SPEAK CLEARLY ENOUGH SO THAT PEOPLE OTHER THAN THEIR OWN FAMILY AND FRIENDS CAN UNDERSTAND THEM EASILY.**

    YES   NOT YET

    ____   ____

22. **UNDERSTAND THE SPEECH OF CHILDREN AND ADULTS OTHER THAN THEIR FAMILY MEMBERS.**

    YES   NOT YET

    ____   ____

23. **UNDERSTAND SIMPLE QUESTIONS AND GIVE SIMPLE ANSWERS.**

    "Do you have John's pencil?"

    "No, this is mine."

    YES   NOT YET

    ____   ____

2. Understanding and Being Understood

Before children start school, it would help if they could

24. FOLLOW SIMPLE DIRECTIONS LIKE WHERE TO SIT, WHERE TO PUT A BOOK, OR WHERE TO THROW A BALL.

YES   NOT YET

———   ———

25. FOLLOW INSTRUCTIONS THAT HAVE TWO OR THREE PARTS.

"Close the door, hang up your coat, and sit down, please."

YES   NOT YET

———   ———

26. TELL SOMEONE HOW THEY ARE FEELING.

	YES	NOT YET
tired	———	———
happy	———	———
sad	———	———
angry	———	———
mixed up	———	———

2. Understanding and Being Understood

Before children start school, it would help if they could

27. ASK FOR WHATEVER THEY NEED.

YES   NOT YET

——   ——

28. TELL A SIMPLE STORY, IN THE RIGHT ORDER, about something that happened that morning, or yesterday, or in the past.

YES   NOT YET

——   ——

For ways parents can help their children speak well enough to be understood by others and understand them, as well, please see A Guide for Parents, *pages 57-59.*

Being ready for school means that children understand what school is about, and why they are there.

First, children need to be able to be away from their parents or people they know for a few hours without being upset. Next, they need to be glad to be going to school, and to be willing and able to do what is expected of them. This means that they understand that they must respect their teachers and learn to follow rules. Finally, they need to be able to get along well with other children , and to know how to do certain things for themselves.

All of these are very important, because how well children do in school, and in the rest of their lives, depends on their being able to do these kinds of things.

3. Self-Help and Social Skills

Before children start school, it would help if they could:

29. **UNDERSTAND THAT IN SCHOOL, CHILDREN ARE EXPECTED TO DO WHAT THEIR TEACHERS ASK.**

    YES   NOT YET

    ____   ____

30. **BE COMFORTABLE BEING AWAY FROM THEIR PARENT OR CAREGIVER, AND WITH NEW ADULTS AND CHILDREN.**

    YES   NOT YET

    ____   ____

31. **KNOW HOW TO WAIT**

    to take turns in games,
    YES   NOT YET

    ____   ____

    their turn to give an answer,
    YES   NOT YET

    ____   ____

    for instructions from the teacher about how and when to begin something.
    YES   NOT YET

    ____   ____

Before children start school, it would help if they could

32. **UNDERSTAND THAT OTHER PEOPLE HAVE RIGHTS AND FEELINGS, JUST AS THEY DO.**

   YES   NOT YET

   ___   ___

33. **MANAGE, AT LEAST SOME OF THE TIME, TO**

   YES   NOT YET

   share the use of toys,   ___   ___

   work together with other children on a task,   ___   ___

   give help to someone when asked,   ___   ___

   resist touching things when asked not to,   ___   ___

   know when to say "please" and "thank you".   ___   ___

3. Self-Help and Social Skills

Before children start school, it would help if they could

34. SIT QUIETLY FOR A WHILE and

play with a toy,

concentrate on a task,

listen to a story.

YES NOT YET

___ ___

___ ___

___ ___

35. PLAY WITH OTHER CHILDREN WITHOUT HAVING A LOT OF FIGHTS.

YES NOT YET

___ ___

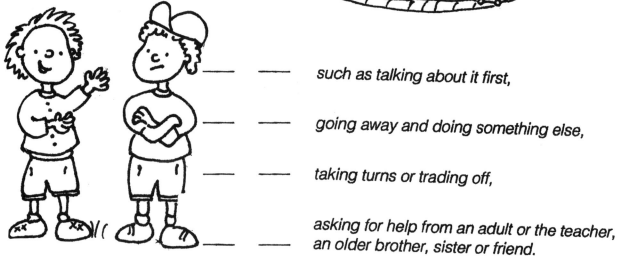

36. KNOW A FEW WAYS TO TRY TO SETTLE ARGUMENTS,

___ ___ *such as talking about it first,*

___ ___ *going away and doing something else,*

___ ___ *taking turns or trading off,*

___ ___ *asking for help from an adult or the teacher, an older brother, sister or friend.*

Before children start school, it would help if they could

37. TAKE OFF AND PUT ON THEIR OUTER CLOTHES THEMSELVES, like jackets and sweaters.

YES   NOT YET

_____   _____

38. TAKE THEMSELVES TO THE BATHROOM, WITHOUT HELP, and remember to wash their hands and flush the toilet, every time.

YES   NOT YET

_____   _____

39. WASH AND DRY THEIR HANDS AND FACE, ALL BY THEMSELVES.

YES   NOT YET

_____   _____

40. FEED THEMSELVES NEATLY USING A SPOON OR FORK.

YES   NOT YET

_____   _____

3. Self-Help and Social Skills

Before children start school, it would help if they could

41. CONTINUE WORKING ON SOMETHING, EVEN WHEN

	YES	NOT YET
it starts to get hard,	——	——
the first try didn't work,	——	——
something happens to distract them.	——	——

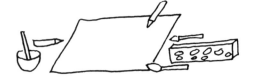

42. FINISH SOMETHING BEFORE STARTING SOMETHING ELSE.

	YES	NOT YET
	——	——

For some ways parents can help their children have self-help and social skills, please see A Guide for Parents, *pages 60-64.*

Before they go to school, children need to have good control over their movements. They need to be able to sit, stand, walk, climb stairs and run when they need to, without hurting themselves, bumping into things or breaking things. In school, they'll be part of a group that's doing these things, and they need to be able to do them, too.

4. Large Movement Skills

Before children start school, it would help if they could

YES   NOT YET

43. WALK WITH EASE. —— ——

44. RUN WITHOUT FALLING FREQUENTLY. —— ——

45. JUMP, USING BOTH FEET AT THE SAME TIME. —— ——

46. HOP ON ONE FOOT A FEW TIMES, without falling.

YES   NOT YET

—— ——

47. BALANCE ON ONE FOOT, for a few seconds.

YES   NOT YET

—— ——

Before children start school, it would help if they could

48. WALK UP STAIRS,
one foot after another.

YES   NOT YET

——   ——

49. WALK DOWN STAIRS,
one foot after the other,
holding the bannister
if they're going really fast,
or the stairs are steep.

YES   NOT YET

——   ——

50. WALK BACKWARDS
FOR SIX OR SEVEN STEPS,
placing toe to heel in a straight line,
without turning to look behind.

YES   NOT YET

——   ——

4. Large Movement Skills

Before children start school, it would help if they could

51. THROW AND CATCH A LARGE BALL,

using both hands.

YES   NOT YET

_____   _____

52. CARRY SOMETHING ON TOP OF SOMETHING ELSE like an apple on a plate.

YES   NOT YET

_____   _____

For some ways that parents can help their child learn large movement skills, please see A Guide for Parents, *pages 65-67.*

Many things children do and learn in school depend on their having good control of their hands and fingers.

In school, there are many new things to touch and do. Children need to know how to use their hands well to do them, and to take care of themselves and their things.

Children need to open and close things, to use things without dropping them, breaking them, or spilling them. They need to be able to hold pencils and crayons correctly so they can learn to write, and do math. If children can't use their hands well, they'll be afraid to try new things, and trying new things is an important way children learn.

5. Small Movement Skills

Before children start school, it would help if they could

53. STIR SOMETHING IN A BOWL,
WITHOUT SPILLING.

        YES   NOT YET

        ——   ——

54. PICK UP A PALM-SIZED BALL AND ROLL
IT ACROSS THE FLOOR OR TABLE.

        YES   NOT YET

        ——   ——

55. STACK 5 BLOCKS ON TOP
OF EACH OTHER.

        ——

56. KNOW HOW TO USE A SPOON
AND FORK, AND MAYBE A KNIFE,
TO EAT WITH, CORRECTLY.

        YES   NOT YET

        ——   ——

57. HOLD A PENCIL OR CRAYON WITH
THEIR THUMB AND FINGERS.

   YES NOT YET

   —— ——

Before children start school, it would help if they could

58. OPEN A SCREW TOP JAR,

	YES	NOT YET
remove the lid,	___	___
put it back on, and	___	___
tighten it again.	___	___

59. OPEN A DOOR BY TURNING THE KNOB.

YES NOT YET

___ ___

60. TURN WATER FAUCETS ON AND OFF.

YES NOT YET

___ ___

61. LACE A SHOELACE THROUGH 3 LARGE BEADS.

YES NOT YET

___ ___

62. CUT WITH A SCISSORS small ones that work.

YES NOT YET

___ ___

5. Small Movement Skills

Before children start school, it would help if they could

63. **DO BUTTONS ON THE FRONT OF THEIR CLOTHES**
and know how to open and close

	YES	NOT YET
snaps,	___	___
buckles,	___	___
zippers.	___	___

64. **TAKE A PINCH OF SALT OR SUGAR OR ANYTHING FINELY GROUND.**

YES	NOT YET
___	___

65. **PICK UP A SMALL BEAN OR PEBBLE**
with thumb and forefinger.

YES	NOT YET
___	___

For some ways parents can help their children learn small movement skills, please see A Guide for Parents, *pages 68-72.*

Although we don't always realize it, we use all our senses to learn things about the world, even things we learn at school.

While we learn a lot through seeing and hearing, we also learn about things from how they FEEL, how they TASTE, and even how they SMELL! Think about how many ways we know it when we wash a dog!!

Using our senses helps us tell when things are ALIKE, and when they're DIFFERENT, which is very important for learning everything, including reading, writing, drawing, music and even arithmetic and science.

So, it's important for children, who have so much to learn, to be able to use all their senses to learn about the things around them.

6. Using All Their Senses

❖ SEEING ❖

Before children start school it would help if they could

66. **SEE DIFFERENCES IN SIZE BETWEEN SIMILAR OBJECTS, AND SAY WHICH IS SMALLER AND WHICH IS LARGER.**

	YES	NOT YET
two friends,one bigger, one smaller,	___	___
two different glasses or pans,	___	___
two different small animals.	___	___

67. **TELL YOU IF TWO COLORS ARE THE SAME OR NOT, and maybe know a few color names, too.**

YES   NOT YET

___   ___

68. **TELL YOU IF TWO SHAPES ARE THE SAME OR NOT, and maybe know what they're called.**

YES   NOT YET

___   ___

69. **LOOK AT YOU FOR A MOMENT, CLOSE THEIR EYES, AND TELL YOU ONE OR TWO THINGS YOU ARE WEARING.**

YES   NOT YET

___   ___

❖ *HEARING* ❖

Before children start school, it would help if they could

70. POINT TO WHERE SOUNDS ARE COMING FROM.

YES   NOT YET

With your child standing still, eyes closed or blindfolded

make sounds behind, in front, and at child's side.

____   ____

71. TELL YOU WHICH OF TWO SOUNDS IS LOUDER, and which softer.

YES   NOT YET

____   ____

72. TELL YOU IF TWO SOUNDS YOU MAKE ARE THE SAME OR DIFFERENT, AND THEN, TELL YOU WHAT THEY ARE.

Try running a little water, then a lot, or

walking toward your child, then away.

YES   NOT YET

____   ____

6. Using All Their Senses

Before children start school, it would help if they could

73. TELL YOU IF TWO WORDS YOU SAY ARE THE SAME OR DIFFERENT, even if they haven't heard them before.

YES   NOT YET

____   ____

74. REPEAT CORRECTLY ALMOST ANY WORD YOU SAY, but no extra long ones.

	YES	NOT YET
simple	____	____
total	____	____
Nevada	____	____

75. REPEAT A SHORT *SENTENCE* CORRECTLY.

YES   NOT YET

____   ____

❖ TASTING AND SMELLING ❖

76. IDENTIFY SOME FAMILIAR FOODS BY TASTE ALONE.

	YES	NOT YET
peanut butter	____	____
a piece of banana or apple	____	____
a crust of bread or chocolate	____	____

Before children start school, it would help if they could,
with their eyes tightly closed or blindfolded,

77. TELL IF TWO SMELLS ARE THE SAME OR DIFFERENT.

                   YES   NOT YET

                   ————— —————

78. IDENTIFY SEVERAL DIFFERENT FOODS BY SMELL ALONE.

                   YES   NOT YET

                   ————— —————

❖ TOUCHING ❖

79. IDENTIFY SOME OBJECTS ONLY BY TOUCH.

	YES	NOT YET
pencil	———	———
spoon	———	———
orange	———	———
apple	———	———
cup	———	———
sock	———	———

80. TELL THE DIFFERENCE BY TOUCH ALONE BETWEEN THINGS THAT FEEL ALIKE.

	YES	NOT YET
a key and a coin	———	———
a spoon and a fork	———	———
an apple and orange	———	———
a cup and a ball	———	———
a sock and a hankerchief	———	———

6. Using All Their Senses

Another sense that's important for learning is body sense: knowing what's happening to one's body, and how to make it do what we want. Our bodies, just as our eyes and ears, also tell us a lot about what's going on. Even with our eyes closed, we need to be able to tell if our arms or legs are bent or straight, if we are standing straight, leaning forward or backward, or if the elevator is going up or down. Children need to know how to get messages from their bodies, too.

Before children start school, it would help if they could

81. IMITATE THE BODY POSTURE AND GESTURES OF ANOTHER PERSON.

    YES   *NOT YET*

    ———   ———

82. TELL YOU IF YOU'VE MOVED THEIR ARMS UP OR DOWN, FORWARD OR BACK WHEN THEIR EYES ARE CLOSED OR BLINDFOLDED.

    YES   *NOT YET*

    ———   ———

83. SAY WHERE THEY ARE BEING TOUCHED WHEN THEIR EYES ARE CLOSED OR BLINDFOLDED.

    YES   *NOT YET*

    ———   ———

For some ways parents can help their children develop all their sensory skills, please see A Guide for Parents, *pages 73–81.*

Children are really not expected to be able to read or write before they start school. But much of what children learn all through school involves pictures of many kinds. Before starting school, it's important that children understand that photographs and drawings in books, magazines, and newspapers can stand for real things, and that real things can be shown in books by drawings and photographs.

7. Recognizing Pictures

Before children start school, it would help if they could

84. IDENTIFY DRAWINGS OR PHOTOS OF COMMON OBJECTS IN BOOKS, NEWSPAPERS, OR MAGAZINES.

YES   NOT YET

___   ___

85. POINT TO A REAL OBJECT AND FIND A PICTURE OF IT IN A BOOK, NEWSPAPER OR MAGAZINE.

YES   NOT YET

___   ___

86. LOOK AT A PICTURE, AND TELL YOU WHAT'S HAPPENING IN IT, OR MAKE UP A STORY ABOUT IT.

YES   NOT YET

___   ___

A SPECIAL NOTE TO PARENTS

Teachers all agree that it is not necessary before kindergarten for children to know how to read or write letters or numbers. However, since much of what children learn in school involves books, reading and writing, it helps them be ready for Kindergarten if they have some ideas about the connection between speaking, writing, and books before they come to school.

8. Words & Letters

Before children start school, it would help if they knew

87. THAT THEIR NAMES, AND THE WORDS FOR EVERYTHING
CAN BE WRITTEN DOWN ON PAPER.

YES   NOT YET

——   ——

88. THAT BOOKS, NEWSPAPERS, LETTERS, MAGAZINES,
AND NOTES ARE WORDS WRITTEN DOWN
AND TELL US THINGS.

——   ——

89. THAT WORDS ARE WRITTEN
DOWN USING *LETTERS*.

——   ——

90. THAT THE LETTERS ARE
CALLED THE *ALPHABET*.

——   ——

91. That *NUMBERS*, LIKE THREE, SIX, AND
TWO CAN ALSO BE WRITTEN DOWN,
WITH *NUMERALS:* 3, 6, AND 2.

——   ——

92. HOW TO HOLD A PENCIL OR CRAYON CORRECTLY
SO THEY CAN MAKE MARKS ON PAPER.

——   ——

93. HOW TO COPY A SIMPLE FIGURE,
like a squiggly line or circle.

——   ——

For some ways parents can help their children learn about words, letters, and pictures, please see A Guide for Parents, *pages 82–86.*

If your child knew many of the things in this checklist, he or she is probably ready to start school and have a good time learning new things.

If there were a number of things your child still needs to learn, the next part of this handbook, **A Guide for Parents,** shows many easy and enjoyable things that parents and other caregivers can do to help children learn them.

A
Guide for
Parents

HOW PARENTS CAN HELP THEIR CHILDREN BE READY FOR SCHOOL

Parents, and the people children spend the most time with, are the people children learn the most from, whether they're trying to teach children or not.

Children are natural learners. They're always learning from whatever is happening around them. They never stop. That's lucky, because *children don't know anything when they're born, and there's a lot they need to learn. That's why they ask so many questions!*

This means that when you and your child are together, *anywhere,* you can teach them everything they need to know from just the ordinary things that happen all the time, using everyday things around the house.

Any parent can do it. You don't need any special equipment, any special training, or even extra time. But there are some important things to remember about teaching children.

HOW TO TEACH THINGS TO CHILDREN

Children have a lot to learn, but don't try to teach them more than one thing at a time.

Don't be surprised or disappointed if they forget some things you tell them, or if some things take longer than you expect. To keep trying,

children need to be encouraged.

Try very hard not to make them feel bad about things they don't yet know or can't yet do. It really helps if you remember to

always praise them for trying, especially when they don't get things perfectly right. *That's when they need it the most.*

When children make mistakes, and we scold them, we shift their attention away from what they were learning to feeling bad about themselves.

Even if it's true, try not to say things like

"No, that's all wrong", or *"Why don't you remember that? I just told you yesterday."*

Children can't say why they don't remember something.

Neither can we: try it yourself sometime!

Scolding changes trying to learn something from being fun to being something that makes children unhappy, and something to avoid.

It's better for them if you say things like

"That was a good try," or

"That's almost right" or

"Good, only this part needs to be changed."

This tells them that what they did wasn't *perfect*, but it encourages them to keep trying. And that's the most important thing of all.

When they're right, and we say *"You're so great!"* or *"You're such a good boy (or girl) for getting that right"* children may be afraid we'll think they're bad or that they let us down when they get something wrong.

That makes them afraid to try things they don't already know.

So, It's better to praise the work or their effort rather than praise the child. They'll feel good, anyway.

It's better to say things like

"You did a really good job with that!", or

"It must feel good to know how to do that!", or

"It's so great that you kept at that 'til you got it."

This tells them that it's fun to know things, and that hard work is admired.

You can help your children learn everything they need to know to be ready for kindergarten just by talking with them about

what things are,

what they're like, and

how things work.

Some of the best things you can do for children are to

read them stories, or tell them your own stories,

let them help you with what you're doing,

let them do things for themselves,

ask them questions, and answer theirs.

REMEMBER, WHEN CHILDREN ASK QUESTIONS, THEY'RE TRYING TO LEARN.

Questions mean children are interested and curious about what's happening around them, and want to learn about it. That's something parents can be happy about. So be patient with their questions, no matter how many they ask!

Every parent, and anyone who spends time with children, can do these things, but they usually don't because such ordinary things don't seem important. But they are.

In fact, just doing these everyday things which make it fun to be together are the best ways to help children get ready for school.

In this guide, you'll find a lot of easy, everyday ways parents and anyone who takes care of children can help them learn everything children need to know to be ready to get the most from their first school experiences.

Doing these simple things is the best way for children to learn and practice what they need to know.

Learning these things helps children to learn even *more*. This helps them feel good about themselves. It helps them like school, and want to do well.

And remember, don't try to do too much. One new thing a day is enough.

TALKING TO CHILDREN

The best way parents, or anyone, can help children learn words, or names, or almost anything they need to know is to

TALK TO THEM,   OFTEN,   ABOUT ALMOST EVERYTHING!

**Children need to be spoken to
as much as they need air,
and love, and food, and sleep.**

Children are never really too young to talk to, because even if they don't catch every word, they're learning to *listen*, and they're learning from you, their most important teacher, that

**THERE ARE WORDS FOR EVERYTHING,
EVEN THINGS WE CAN'T SEE!**

They're also learning that words
are one of the most important ways
people connect with each other.

**Parents seldom realize that just talking to children, and getting them
to talk to you, is probably the most important thing they can do for them.**

Children love it when you talk
to them. It makes them feel
important and grown-up.
They learn more than you think,
and every parent can do it.

The way you talk doesn't have
to be anything special. Just
speak clearly, the way you,
and other people, usually talk.

**Be sure not to use baby talk
when you speak to your
child, and ask other people
not to do it, too. Baby talk
makes it harder, not easier,
for your child to learn to
speak so other people will
understand him or her.**

Whenever you're together, in the house or out, everywhere,

there's *always something* you can point out;

there's *always something* interesting for a child to learn about.

YOU CAN START BY TALKING ABOUT THE CHILD.

Tell him or her words for the different parts of themselves, from head to toe.

Start by seeing how many body words your child **already** knows.

Let your child know how pleased you are that he or she knows some, already.

Try to use these new *body* words in things you tell

your child to do. You can do it in funny ways.

"Rita, bring me the milk, please, but don't use your elbows."

> **Remember, don't try to teach more than one or two new words on the same day. Repeat them the next day. It's a good idea, each day, to ask about things you talked about the day before. That way you go over them, and tie them to new things. This helps your child learn the new things as well as remember the old.**

WHEN YOU'RE OUT IN THE STREET, OR ANYWHERE,

you can point out things around you:

> **stores, dogs,**
>
> **trees, houses,**
>
> **signs, cars**.

Ask your child to tell you what they're called.

If he doesn't know, it's alright.
Just tell him what it's called.

> Ask your child to tell you what she knows about things.

Don't make children feel bad if they don't know much yet.
After all, that's why you're talking about it together.

In addition to talking about what things are and what they're called, ask your child what makes them look different or special:

> you can talk about how things *feel*,
>
> how they *look*, how they *sound*,
>
> and even how they *smell*.

TALKING TO CHILDREN is also how they learn words about:

what things are like (*red or green, hot or cold, big or small*)

how things move (*quickly or slowly*),

where things are (*close, far away, on top, under, over, first or last*),

when things happen (*yesterday, today, before, after, now, soon, later, tomorrow*).

> **The two of you will have a good time together, and your child will be learning important things from his or her first and best teacher.**

The Opposites Game is a lot of fun to play. You can do it everywhere, and anytime.

Ask your child something like *"What's the opposite of hot?"*

Your child may not know what 'opposite' means, so start with a few examples, like 'big and little', or 'up and down'.

To be sure he or she understands, ask your child to tell you some opposites, first.

After that, you'll be able to have fun playing the game together anywhere.
And don't forget, after you ask a few, it's your child's turn to ask the questions.

NAME GAMES are also something you can do with your child anywhere.

You can start by pointing to things around the house. Ask your child, *"Sandra, is this the refrigerator or the stove?"*

Then, see how many things your child can point to, or name by herself.

COUNTING how many things your child can name helps to teach your child something about numbers, too.

WHEN YOU TAKE YOUR CHILD TO THE STORE

or the doctor,

to the clinic, the church, or the bank,

tell him or her what happens at these places,

who these people are,

and what these people do.

Any place you might be, you can take turns playing a guessing game.

You say, **"I see (or I'm thinking about) something white and cold, and you drink it."**

Have your child try to guess what it is.
To make it harder, add another word, like 'sweet'.

Each change makes it very different, doesn't it?
Then ask your child to describe something for YOU to guess.

TALK TO CHILDREN ABOUT ALL KINDS OF EVERYDAY THINGS, as they happen.

TALK ABOUT WHAT YOU'RE DOING.

What clothes you're wearing (my light blue jacket).

What foods you're eating (bread and tomatoes).

Where you're going *("Let's go home, it's time to eat.")*.

TALK about what you're *thinking* of doing later, or tomorrow, or what you did yesterday, or long ago, when you were little, too.

Then ask your child to try it, too.

CHILDREN LEARN A LOT IF YOU TALK ABOUT *WHY* YOU'RE DOING SOMETHING, TOO.

Why you made one decision rather than the other,

Why you chose one sweater rather then the other,

Why you took the bus instead of walking.

It helps them learn how to make decisions, too.

HAVING SOME IDEAS ABOUT HOW MUCH AND HOW MANY is very helpful for the arithmetic that children will be taught in school.

This means understanding something about things that are **bigger** and **smaller** than each other, and that some things that have **more,** and others **less.**

For example, you can start by pointing out that YOU are BIGGER and HE or SHE is SMALLER.

You can also do this with pairs of things. Anything around the house will be fine.

Ask your child which of two things around you is bigger and which is smaller.

Use things with big differences first.

If you're outside, ask your child about

two different houses,

or two different trees.

Then gradually, use things

closer and closer in size (two different jars).

When he or she can do that, **ask your child** to find things that are bigger and smaller than each other, without your pointing to them first.

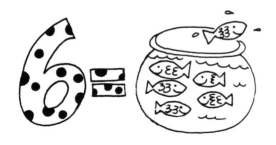

Having some ideas about how much and how many also means having some simple ideas about **counting,** and how **number words,** like "**two**" and "**four**" and "**six**" mean different **amounts of things.**

COUNTING GAMES, and funny ones, too, can be played anywhere.

You can help your child get ideas about numbers and amounts anyplace you might be.

There are things to count everywhere.

You can ask your child to count things like

buttons on a shirt,   people in a waiting room,

legs on a table,   keys on a chain.

A good counting game is to see how many different things you can find to say about just one thing,

a person, a toy, or even just a fork.

Start by doing it yourself,
and then ask your child to do it.

This helps your child learn to notice things, too.

Waiting for a bus, you can count how many people are also waiting.

If the bus has a simple number, you can point it out.

Then ask your child to tell you if he or she sees that number in other places, too.

In line at the supermarket, you can count how many people are in your line.

Then, count how many there are in *the other line.*

You can count how many things there are in your basket.

Point out which person is FIRST, who is SECOND, and who is THIRD.

This gives your child some ideas about the ORDER of things.

When your child has learned to count a few objects you can show him or her how these numbers are *written* down.

Point out these written numbers, called *numerals*, wherever you see them.

Ask your child to point them out to you, too:

on price tags

on houses

at the gas station

on license plates.

They're everywhere,

which makes them very important to know about!

It's good for children to start to learn something about money, and what it's for. Let children see you pay for things using money.

Let them handle money, and pay for things themselves sometimes. Show them the differences in coins, and tell them what they're called.

When parents, and others who care for children, use ordinary things in the world around them to help children learn, it's like using a magic wand to turn a child's everyday world into an exciting and interesting place, and themselves into children's best teachers. You'll think of many good things to do, yourself.

To be ready for school, and learn what they'll be taught, children need to be able to understand what other people say to them. They also need to speak clearly so that other people can understand them, too.

Listen to your child speak as if you never met him or her before. Closing your eyes helps.

Be honest: are there ways he or she says things, or uses special words, that only you and the family understand?

If so, help your child listen to how other people say these words, and practice saying these with your child until other people can understand him or her.

Never scold children or make them feel bad about the way they talk. Do make sure you say things clearly and correctly, so they can hear how to do it. Sometimes, ask them to try to say something your way.

Let them know you've noticed each time they say things even a little more clearly, and how pleased you are they tried. It's hard to change the way you say things all at once.

THERE ARE MANY WAYS PARENTS CAN HELP CHILDREN SPEAK CLEARLY.

Give your child short messages to deliver for you:

"Daddy wants to know where his keys are."

Ask your child to tell you what the person who got the message said.

"Mommy says they're where you left them."

Let children talk and listen to other people on the phone sometimes.

Listening to other people on TV and the radio gives them a chance to hear the way other people speak.

Ask them to **repeat what someone said or tell you what the program was about.**

That way they have to **listen,** they have to try to **remember** what they heard, and they practice **talking** about it.

When children ask questions, it also helps if you answer questions with more than just *"YES"* or *"NO",* even when that might really be enough.

Try to include some explanation about why things are happening.

"Is Anna coming?"

"No, Anna is not coming to see us today. She had to go to work. She'll come Sunday."

Encourage your CHILD to answer that way, too.

"Did you go to the park with your class today?"

"No, we didn't. The weather was bad."

Understanding what people say depends on listening and remembering.

TRY PLAYING THE ECHO GAME.

Say something short and funny, (but slowly and correctly). Then ask your child to repeat it several times.

"The crayon ate the teacher's chalk."

Sometimes, try to use words your child might be having some trouble saying. This game gives your child practice in listening, remembering, and saying words correctly.

You can help your child learn to listen and remember when you play THE INSTRUCTION GAME.

Tell your child three things to do, one at a time.

Make them simple, funny, and not at all logical.

"Okay, Sammy, FIRST, clap your hands,

THEN, walk to the door, and

THIRD, get some milk from the refrigerator".

Don't point or make any gestures.

When your child can remember three instructions, try four.

BE PATIENT, AND ENCOURAGING.

Then, let them make up instructions for you, or their friends, to follow.

> If you think that your child's speech could be a problem, talk to a doctor or nurse, or a teacher, and ask about getting some help. The school your child will go to will be glad to talk to you about it, and help.
>
> IT'S ONE OF THE BEST THINGS YOU CAN DO TO HELP YOUR CHILD DO WELL AND BE HAPPY IN SCHOOL.

> Being able to do things for one's self, to get along with others, and to be able to be away from people one knows, are basic to being ready to go to school. If your child isn't able to do this yet, parents and those who look after them are the best people to help them learn.

If children haven't yet spent much time with other children and grownups, away from their parents and people they're used to, help them learn this before they go to school. Here are some things you can do:

Try to arrange times for them to play with other children as much as possible. Invite other children to visit.

Take turns with other people you know to have *your* child visit *them* as well, but not for too long at first.

Arrange for your child to play with other children in a place outside your own home, such as a playschool, with another adult in charge. Help your child get used to your not being there, a little longer each time.

Have the other children bring toys so they can learn how to

SHARE,

TRADE OFF, and

TAKE TURNS, because

SHARING, TRADING OFF, and TAKING TURNS are things they need to learn to do instead of fighting.

It's important for children to know that they have to do what some other grownups, like teachers, tell them, too.

PLAYING SCHOOL WITH YOUR CHILD
can help him or her learn what
will be expected in school.

Knowing what is expected and what
to expect makes it easier for your child
when school begins.

**Reading a story to a group of children
sitting in a circle is a good way to do this.**

> You can ask them questions about
> the story and how they liked it.

> That way, they can learn to raise
> their hands and wait to be called on.

> Having a few other children around
> makes it more like a real school.

Children can take turns playing teacher, too. Boys as well as girls should be
encouraged to do this. A teacher is a very important person.

**Another important thing you can do to help your child
is to talk about things that can't be seen.**

Talk to your child about how you're
FEELING:

cold,

tired,

hungry,

happy,

sad,

or funny in the stomach.

Ask your child to tell you how he or she is feeling, too.

One of the most important things for parents to remember is to try not to do things for children which they can do, or *could* learn to do for themselves.

Lots of us think that being a good parent means doing **everything** for our children. But it depends on what **kinds of** things we do. It's not good to keep children from learning to do certain things for themselves.

Being a good parent means helping your children grow strong and teaching them to do as many things for themselves as possible.

Children really love to feel they can do things. It makes them feel important and grown up.

Sometimes, parents tend to do more things for their boys than their girls. That really doesn't help either the boys *or* the girls feel strong and smart. In school they'll feel ashamed of not knowing how to do what is expected or what the other children know how to do.

There are many things, like those in this book, that parents can do for children to help them grow strong, and be ready to do well in kindergarten.

SO, TEACH YOUR CHILD TO DO SOME THINGS WITHOUT YOUR HELP.

Of course, it sometimes takes longer that way. But in the end it's worth it, because your child has learned something.

When children ask you to do something they need to be able to do on their own,

ask them to begin doing it alone.

Tell them that when they can't get any further, you'll be there to help.

Let children know how much you like it when they try to do things for themselves.

Be sure to notice, and encourage them when they try something they haven't done before.

Some important things that you can help them to learn are:

    putting on and taking off their own clothes,

    **taking themselves to the toilet
(and remembering to flush it,
and wash their hands every time),**

    washing and drying their hands and face,

    combing their hair and brushing their teeth,

    **making a snack for themselves, and
putting their things away.**

Being able to put on and take off their own clothes, and close them up after going to the toilet are very important in school.

Children feel good if they can do these things before they go to kindergarten, and very bad when they don't.

So parents should be sure to give them the chance to practice doing buttons and zippers on their own clothes. They can even practice on clothes that no one's wearing.

IT'S VERY GOOD FOR CHILDREN IF YOU LET THEM HELP YOU WITH WHATEVER YOU'RE DOING.

If you're making dinner, both boys and girls can

take things out of the refrigerator or closets,

put the dishes, knives and forks at everyone's place, (this is a good time for counting things, too),

put the glasses on the table, or

fold napkins.

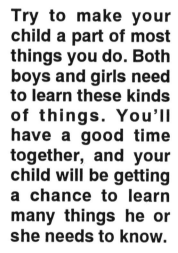

A very important thing you can do to help children be ready for school is to encourage them to finish something before starting something else.

> Try to make your child a part of most things you do. Both boys and girls need to learn these kinds of things. You'll have a good time together, and your child will be getting a chance to learn many things he or she needs to know.

A good way to help with this is to tell them *that you notice it each time they stick to something even a little longer than usual.*

If you let children know you appreciate their trying, they'll try all the more.

Children learn and master movement skills at different times.

It's not a good idea to compare your child's skill at anything with another child's. Children have their own pace, and fast isn't always better.

But it is good to give children the chance to practice them as much as possible. These skills are learned, and practice is important in everything we learn.

Remember, using patience and praise, you can be a child's best teacher.

The games children play for fun, like

skipping rope,

riding trikes,

throwing balls,

ping-pong, or

baseball,

are the natural ways children learn these large movement skills.

Do whatever you can to help both boys and girls get a chance to play these games.

If you don't live where there are steps to go up or down, or room outside to run or throw or kick a ball, look around you for ways to help your child get a chance to do these things.

IF YOU PASS A SMALL FLIGHT OF STEPS, take a few moments to let your child go up and down them a few times if they want to (they usually do).

ASKING YOUR CHILD TO COUNT THE STEPS teaches something important, too.

TAKE A FEW MOMENTS, if you can spare them, to let children walk along a low wall, or jump from one crack in the sidewalk to another. Be sure you let *girls* know it's alright to do this, too.

It takes longer to get to where you're going, so don't do it unless you have the time.

If your child likes dancing or marching to music around the house, encourage him or her to do it. Marching and dancing help them learn to use their bodies safely. They also help children develop a sense of rhythm, which is important in learning many other things as well.

Another game you can play together, in a park or someplace where there are no cars and not too many people, is to walk, and take turns in kicking a large ball ahead of you.

You'll both have fun,

get some good exercise,

and your child will have

the chance to develop

important movement skills.

A good way for children to learn to balance and carry a couple of things that are stacked on top of each other is to let them bring or take things to the table.

Be sure you give them things that won't slide or spill, or cause problems if they get dropped.

Let children help you carry packages, or pick up two or three things at a time and carry them someplace for you.

Don't let them take too many things, like this child, who can't see where he's going!

Getting things off the super-market shelves for you is another way your child can learn to handle a few things at a time without dropping them.

Doing these things gives children the chance to touch things and move them around when it's allowed, because they're helping.

Being helpful makes them feel good about themselves, too.

When you check out, let children help you take things out of the basket and put them on the counter.

Doing simple, everyday things like these helps children learn more than you'd ever imagine!

Doing things well with their hands is important for many things children will learn in school, especially for writing. Children need a lot of practice to get their fingers to do what they want. This is the time to *encourage* children to touch things!

The best toys to help children learn to do things well with their hands are the ordinary things all around the house.

ONE VERY SPECIAL THING YOU HAVE TO MAKE SURE YOU HAVE HOWEVER, IS PATIENCE. Expect them to do things slowly, and to need to do them many times.

Remember to encourage children and praise them for TRYING, especially when they don't do things exactly right.

Children can get good practice, and learn to do things well with their hands just by helping you do whatever you're doing in the house, or anyplace else.

For example, as often as you can, let them help you

open the mail,

put things away,

clean things in the house,

Try to think of some part of what you're doing that your child could safely do, even though it's faster to do it yourself!

STIRRING SOMETHING in a glass, a bowl, or a pot is something children love to do. Doing it without spilling or splashing takes a lot of practice.

At first, give them a bowl or glass *with just a little water in it.*

Next time, you can let them try to stir something that has a little *more* water.

PRACTICE IS WHAT THEY NEED, TOO, TO LEARN TO FEED THEMSELVES NEATLY WITH A FORK AND SPOON.

The best, and *safest,* place for them to learn this is at home, where people will be *patient with them and encourage them, even if they make mistakes.*

OPENING AND CLOSING JARS, and getting the lids on straight is not as easy as it seems. It's a very good thing to let children practice this. Learning to write uses the same skills.

Getting the chance to do this many times is the only way children can be sure to learn it.

If your child needs to practice this, save different kinds of jars and bottles and their covers.

Let your child wash and dry these, and then let her match them up with their covers, and screw them on and off. When he or she can do this easily, take the next step.

Fill them with water, and let your child practice opening and closing them without spilling.

The sink is the best place for this. Doing this gives your child practice,too, in turning the water faucets on and off, and you get a chance to try to teach 'left' from 'right,' and 'empty' and 'full'.

LET THEM HELP YOU OPEN OTHER THINGS, TOO.

Milk cartons (they can practice on the closed side of empty ones you fill with water),

juice cans, boxes, letters, all give children practice in small movement skills.

AS ALWAYS, THEY NEED PRACTICE, PATIENCE and PRAISE.

CHILDREN LOVE TO USE KEYS,
and that's a great way for them to get practice with their fingers.

Sometimes, when you don't mind waiting, let them try to open the door using your key.

REMEMBER, though: their fingers aren't very strong, and it's much more difficult from down below to turn the key hard enough to open the door. They'll need practice and encouragement, particularly when they don't get it right at first.

Be sure not to do this when you're in a hurry, or just don't feel like waiting.

CUTTING WITH A SMALL SCISSORS, the kind with round tips, is something that children love to do, and it's very good practice for their fingers.

Newspapers, magazines, and flyers from the supermarkets are great for this. There are lots of brightly colored things in the Sunday paper, too, and you can talk about the colors and the pictures at the same time.

Cutting things out can be an easy game. But be sure the scissors work, and that children use them carefully.

To make cutting things out more interesting, ask your child to find only certain *kinds* of things, like pictures of foods, or cars, or things to wear: things that *go together* in some way.

Doing this will help your child start to learn about
the different ways things can go together.

Folding a piece of paper a few times, making some cuts on the folded side, and then opening it up can be a big surprise, and interesting for both of you.

Children can get good practice in some of the skills they need to learn to write by drawing shapes, like circles and squares on newspaper, old envelopes, wrapping paper or grocery bags.

YOU DRAW THE SHAPES FIRST. Then, ask your child to trace around your marks with a crayon. Then let him or her cut them out with scissors.

LET THEM LACE UP THEIR SNEAKERS OR SHOES and try to tie them.

They get to be good with their hands, as well as learn to dress themselves, if you **let them try to do their buttons and zippers and to snap and unsnap things for themselves.**

You could let them help dress the younger children, if you have any.

All this takes longer at first, and sometimes it's really hard to hold back and wait, but once children learn these things, they are very proud of themselves, and eager to learn more.

LET CHILDREN HELP YOU COOK.

The kitchen is one of the best classrooms a child can have. Of course, you have to be careful, but there are many interesting things that children can do there that are safe and help them learn to use their hands and fingers well. Children love to do useful things, just as you do, and you'll both have fun.

Letting children add a pinch of salt or spice to a dish while you are preparing it makes them feel important, and is good practice for their fingers.

Stirring, pouring, opening boxes and closing jars are safe things that children can do that help them practice using their hands and fingers. You'll think of many other things they can do, too.

Be sure you give boys as well as girls the chance to do things in the kitchen. Don't leave them out. They'll enjoy it. Everyone needs to learn how to cook!

The games and things to do together in this section help children use all their senses to learn about things. They can be some of the most enjoyable things you and your child do together. Like everything else in this book, no special toys or equipment are needed.

What you *always* need are the same three 'p's:

PRACTICE   PATIENCE   and   PRAISE.

SEEING GAMES

Seeing differences between things, and understanding what same and different mean, is important for learning many things in school and in life.

For example, being able to see the difference between big things and small ones is very important for learning to read and write.

Seeing differences in shapes and colors is also important for learning math, geography, even science later on.

It is also important to see that things can be the same in some ways, and different in others.

You can help your child learn to see differences by doing things like this:

Teaching Big And Small.

Put a few objects on the table.

First use objects with big differences between them, like a bottle, a cup and some coins.

Ask your child to show you the biggest one, and then the smallest.

If your child can't do this yet, *don't scold or look disappointed.*

Show your child which is biggest and smallest, again and again, until he or she always gets it right.

Then make the differences smaller, and use a few more objects, like

a jar top, two pennies, a dime, a quarter.

Once your child can always tell you which is the biggest and smallest, ask him to put them IN ORDER, from the biggest to the smallest.

Add a few objects, or take them away, and ask your child to arrange them again.

This is a very hard game, so be patient.

Teaching Same And Different.

Another time you can ask your child whether any *two* things are the same or different.

Whatever your child says, "same" or "different", ask your child to tell you *why*.

Don't say anything about whether *you* think it's right or not.

If your child says "same", ask him or her to tell you what is the same.

If your child says "different", ask what is different about them.

Praise your child for whatever she sees as same or different, even if it's not perfectly right, and even if she can't explain it very well.

It is very hard to do this, and you want to encourage your child to keep trying, and to keep noticing things.

If you think your child might be ready, try to talk with him or her about how things can be **different in some ways** (one's big, the other's small) and the **same in others** (they're both apples).

If this seems to confuse your child even a little, stop it and wait until your child is older before you try again.

Seeing Differences In Colors

COLOR GAMES can be played everywhere:

while waiting for a bus,
standing in line,
taking a walk in the park,
or even in a waiting room.

Children enjoy them very much, and learn things they need to know.

YOU CAN TEACH YOUR CHILD TO SEE COLOR DIFFERENCES by pointing to any two things, almost anywhere.

Tell your child when two colors are the *same*, and when they're *different*.
Do this many times until he gets the idea.

Then ask your child to tell you if two things are the same color, or are different colors.

Don't try to teach color **names** until he is always knows if the colors are the **same or different.**

After your child has learned to **see differences** in colors, tell him or her the color name of **one** thing. **"This chair is dark green."**

When you teach your child a new color name ask your child how many things of the same color he or she can find.

Your child pays attention to just one color, and looks for it many times.

That's a good way to learn something.

It helps if you use color names often when you speak to your child.

WHEN YOUR CHILD IS GETTING DRESSED, ask for the names of the colors of the clothes he or she is wearing, and the colors you're wearing, too.

"Wanda, do you want your blue sweater or your red jacket?"

"Tony, please bring me the magazine with the light green cover. It's on the black table."

ANOTHER TIME, ON A SHOPPING TRIP, or on the bus, or in a store, ask your child to name ALL THE COLORS she sees.

And one thing a day is enough, remember?

LEARNING TO SEE DIFFERENCES BETWEEN SHAPES is important for learning to read and write.

So is learning to draw them, and knowing what they're called.

Using a crayon and newspaper, help your child draw outlines around the bottoms of bottles, or boxes, or any other objects.

Then remove them and ask her to *match* the outline to the object.

Ask which shapes are the same, and which are different.
Tell your child what they're called.

Your child will be very pleased to learn that she drew a "SQUARE" or a "CIRCLE", or a "TRIANGLE", when she never even heard those WORDS before!

BEING ABLE TO REMEMBER WHAT YOU SEE IS ALSO IMPORTANT.

Remembering what you see, and noticing changes and differences, are very helpful for learning to read, and even for learning math and science later on.

Here are some games you can play anywhere. They take only seconds, but help your child practice remembering what he or she saw.

The Inside Eye

When you're waiting somewhere with your child, in a clinic or a store, ask your child to close her eyes, and, using *The Inside Eye*, tell you what she saw there. See if your child can name one thing the first few times, two the next, and so on.

> Another way to play this is to ask your child to look around, and then close her eyes. When your child's eyes are closed, change something, quietly, of course.

> Open your shirt collar, or close it. Move something around on the table or take something off it. Then, ask your child to open her eyes, and see if she can tell you what's different.

Be very encouraging. it's not as easy as you think. Try it yourself!

HEARING GAMES

KNOWING IF *SOUNDS* ARE ALIKE OR DIFFERENT is important in learning how to read, as well as in speaking correctly.

So playing hearing games helps your child do well in school. Here are a few.

Wherever you might be, have your child close her eyes tightly, sit still and just listen.

Then ask your child to tell you *all the sounds*, one by one, that she is hearing.

Ask where they're coming from.

Be sure to show your child how impressed you are at how many sounds she recognizes.

Another good game is to say two words, like *slippery* and *stop*.

Ask your child if they were the same words or different ones.

Do this with pairs of words, until he or she is always right.

Sometimes use the same word, sometimes different ones.

Then, ask if they *started* with the same sound, or different ones.

At first, you can repeat them once, but only until your child understands the game.

Learning to listen is important in this game.

Always start with easy words so your child will be encouraged.

Remember: even if she is not always right, praise your child for trying.

Sometimes, you can ask your child to imitate you when you say things.

Use short sentences, at first. "*I want some coffee.*"

Make them silly sometimes, for fun.

"*The monkey served my shoes over rice.*"
Make them a little longer and harder, gradually.

Then change your voice.
Say some things loudly, some softly, some fast, some slowly.

Use a high voice, and a low one,

a happy voice and then a sad one.

Make it easy....at first. And silly is *always* good.

Give your child "credits" by counting how many she can do.

Counting, and writing down how many teaches other ideas that are important for your child to learn.

TASTING AND SMELLING GAMES

The "Mystery Object"

When you're making dinner, or are just in the house together, ask your child to close his or her eyes (tightly).

Then put a piece of food, or a flower, or even a pencil or toy under your child's nose and ask her to guess what "the mystery object" is, just from smelling it. (No touching.)

Another "mystery" game starts with closed eyes, but an open mouth! Place a small bit of food on your child's tongue or lips.

Before letting your child open his eyes, ask your child to name the "mystery food".

Be sure it's something familiar, so your child will be right and experience success the first time. Also, be sure it's nothing hot, too hard or large.

TOUCHING GAMES

You can play this game anywhere. Again, have your child close his eyes, or use a blindfold. Place his hand on a familiar object: a doorknob, a chair, or the family pet.

Then, ask your child to tell you what it is, and how it feels.

It makes it harder to guess when you can't move your hand, so allow this, at first. Later, make your child tell you what it is without moving his hand.

Both you and your child will be surprised by how many things he or she already knows by touch alone.

You can also take a large paper bag,

and **put just two objects in it:**

a **key** and a **coin,**

or a **sock** and a **washcloth,**

or a **big spoon** and a **small one,**

or an **orange** or an **apple.**

First, ask your child to tell you if they're the same or different, and HOW they're the same or different.

After that, let your child take them out and look at them.

Then, put five or six different things in the bag, and, with his or her eyes closed, have your child tell you what they are.

Some other time, when you're both unpacking the groceries after shopping,

have your child reach in the bag and, without looking into it, tell you what things are there *before taking them out of the bag.*

You can ask your child if he or she can turn on the old 'inside eye', and try to remember the color of the object, as well.

BODY SENSE GAMES

Here are some simple things parents can do to help children understand what their bodies tell them, and know when they're up or down, coming or going, leaning or straight.

Ask your child to:

imitate your movements and gestures,

imitate someone in a picture,

play 'statues' with another child.

Doing these things in front of a mirror can help your child compare his or her body to the other person's, and learn how these different positions *feel from the inside.*

Another time, ask your child to close his or her eyes (or use a blindfold).

Then, you or another child can touch your child on the cheek, or hand, the neck, or knee, and ask your child to tell you where she was touched.

If your child doesn't yet know the name of that part, ask your child to show you *where* she was touched.

Then tell your child what that part is called.

Another game that won't take a moment: ask your child to close her eyes, and then move your child's arms or legs up or down, or tilt her head to the side.

Then, ask your child where her arms are, or how her head looks.

Although children are not expected to read or write before kindergarten, much of what children will be learning all through school involves pictures, words, books, reading and writing. A good way to start getting children interested in books is with the pictures.

Helping children understand and learn from pictures.

Here's an easy thing to do that's also fun.
Just doing this helps children learn important things about pictures *(and books)*:

Show your child a picture in the room,
or from a book, magazine or, newspaper,
and ask him to

tell you what things are in the picture,

tell you what's happening in it, or

make up his own story about it.

**Be encouraging, even if you don't agree.
After all, it's your child's story!**

**Another thing that's fun is to ask your child
to show you something in the room that's in a picture.**

Then *you* can point to something in the room and ask *your child* to find something like it in the picture.

Sometimes, point to something in the picture, and see if your child can find something like it in the room.

HELPING CHILDREN LEARN ABOUT BOOKS.

Helping children understand what books are all about is one of the best things anyone can do for children.

Reading to children is one of the best ways to do this.

Children love stories.

They learn some of the most important things they need to know from having stories read to them.

Telling them stories is wonderful, too.

By reading stories to children, you're teaching them very important ideas, without even trying. When you read to children, they're learning

that there are interesting things inside books,

to use their imagination,

that words make us think about things,

that words can give us pictures in our heads, and

that stories can give us ideas we hadn't thought about before.

Reading stories to children also teaches them

that words and ideas can be written down,

that marks on paper stand for the words we use and the sounds we make,

and that these are written down using "letters."

Reading stories to children is one of the best ways to help children be ready for school.

Reading stories to children helps them become interested in books, and eager to learn to read themselves.

They learn important things from having stories read to them, and they love the time you spend together.

Show your child that there are things to be read *everyplace.*

Read simple things to them from newspapers, magazines, signs, even cans of food and cereal boxes. This shows them how important it is to know how to read.

Things To Do With Stories.

Whether you read stories to your children, or tell them your own, there are some ways to do it that make it even more fun, and teach them even more. For example, you can

get your child involved in the story.

While you're reading the story to your child, stop and ask your child

why something happened,

how he would feel if that happened, and

what she thinks will happen next.

Another thing you can do is to

ask your child to make up a different ending.

Be encouraging, and you'll hear some interesting stories yourself!

Once in a while, if a story is not too long, **ask your child to tell the story back to you as best he or she can.**

Don't expect your child to remember everything, so don't scold if things are left out. Praise your child for whatever he remembers.

If your child gets stuck telling you the story, you can help by asking,

"And what happened after that?" or
"What came next?"

Remember, what counts is that your child gets the chance to see what books and pictures are all about, and that you have fun doing these things together.

> **Reading stories to children helps them learn the most important thing they need to know about reading and writing in order to be ready to go to school; that words are written down so that people can tell each other things that are important to them.**

About writing

Sometimes parents try to teach their children to recognize and even write some letters of the alphabet before they go to kindergarten. That can be fun, if your child is eager to learn it, or it can be hard on both of you, and it's not really necessary.

Most teachers don't expect parents to do this. *Teachers* expect to teach children to write in school.

Teachers don't depend on you to teach children to write, but they *do* need you to do some other things.

Teachers need parents to understand that children's education starts long before they come to school.

This means that parents, and others who care for children, are their first, and in some ways their most important, teachers.

Parents are the best people to teach children the things that help them be ready for school and happy to go. Teachers want parents to know this, and to know how much it matters to them and to the children!

Teachers want parents to understand what kinds of things help children be ready for school, and to help them by doing the kinds of everyday things in this Guide.

Children learn best from the ordinary things around them, and simple, everyday experiences which let them see things and do things. These ordinary things can be very exciting when you start to think about them.

Teachers also want parents to know that even after children enter school, parents will still be the most important people in their children's education.

Most of all, teachers need parents to take THE NEXT STEP, right along with their children.

Your child is very lucky to have a parent who cares enough about his or her education to have reached these last pages!

But this part of the Handbook is not about an ending:

IT'S ABOUT A NEW BEGINNING.

Sometimes, parents feel that once their child has started school, their job is finished.

BUT THAT'S NOT THE WAY IT IS.

PARENTS ARE MORE IMPORTANT NOW THAN THEY'VE EVER BEEN!

First, the things that only parents can do, like making sure that their child stays healthy,

gets enough sleep,

eats the right kind of food,

gets to school,

and gets to school on time,

are extremely important to how well children do in school.

If someone doesn't make sure these happen, children won't do as well in school as they could, no matter how wonderful their teachers are.

Second, when their children enter school, parents become important in their children's education in other ways, too.

It is true that your child will be learning some special things in school that the teachers are there to teach them,

but the fact is your child

needs your help more than ever now.

THE SINGLE MOST IMPORTANT INFLUENCE IN HOW WELL YOUR CHILD WILL DO IN SCHOOL IS HOW MUCH YOU STAY INVOLVED IN THE EDUCATION OF YOUR CHILD. IT SHOWS THAT YOU CARE.

No matter how good your child's teachers are, both your child, and his or her teachers, need some things only you can give.

There are many reasons for this.

For many children, entering school can seem like entering a whole new world, that's very different from their home.

When this happens, children can feel very insecure and uncertain about how to act.

Nothing makes children feel better

than seeing a friendly, respectful relationship

between the most important grownups in their lives:

their parents and their teachers.

It's like building a special bridge that
connects school and home:
it makes it easier for him or her to move
back and forth between them.

But even when there isn't a big difference between school and home, just making this kind of contact shows both your child and his or her teacher *that you care about your child's education.*

This has a big effect, and a very good one, on both of them.

But sometimes, parents feel nervous about meeting their child's teacher.

They may have been scared of teachers when they were in school, and even now, they feel too shy and nervous to call and write before the teacher does.

They may feel that the teacher knows **everything** about how to teach their child, and that they have nothing to add.

BUT THE TEACHER DOESN'T FEEL THAT WAY.

Teachers have a hard job. They want any kind of help you can give.

They *need* your help to provide a good education for your child, and they *want* your help in solving any problems that might come up.

After all, you know your child better than anyone else does.

Sharing what you know makes their job easier, and helps them do a better job for your child.

Teachers really appreciate whatever help you can give them!

If you start making contact with the school and teachers *from the beginning, when your child first starts school*, it will get easier all the time.

There are many ways to do this.

MOST SCHOOLS HAVE A KINDERGARTEN VISITING DAY BEFORE CLASSES START.

They send out invitations to the parents of children who will be entering kindergarten the next school year.

Going to this visiting day is a good way to begin.

Other parents will be there, too. You won't be the only one.

Some will be there for the first time, just like you, and maybe feeling a little nervous, too.

It's good to get to know a few parents of your child's classmates.

The school might make a list of everyone's names and phone numbers. That's useful to have.

Find out the name of the principal, too, and write down the school's phone number on the list if it's not there.

Attach this list to some place in the house out in the open, and where it's really easy to find.

Then, when you want to call, you won't have to look up the school's number.

The first time you visit the school, make sure to introduce yourself to your child's teacher. The teacher is eager to meet you, too.

Spend a few minutes talking to him or her and you'll feel much more comfortable the next time. Then, you won't feel so shy about calling the teacher, when you have a question.

This is a good time, too, to mention any special needs your child might have.

It may surprise you, but just this simple thing brings your child and the teacher closer, and makes your child someone special to the teacher.

It's also a good time for you and your child to walk around the school together. Then you'll both feel more at home the next time.

If you miss that first visiting day meeting, you can phone the school and leave a message that you want to know about the next one. The teacher will appreciate it very much.

Your child's teachers will always be glad to hear from you in any way that's easiest for you.

A short note or phone call to ask about how your child is doing, or to let the teacher know if there's anything special happening at home will be very much appreciated. Just returning the teacher's notice will be fine.

This will let the teacher know you're there, and that you care.

When there's a good connection between parents and school,

EVERYONE BENEFITS.

Your *child* will do better,

you learn a lot about how parents can be the most important people in their children's success at school, and the *teacher* can do a better job.

NOW YOUR CHILD WILL HAVE A TEAM OF PEOPLE WITH THE SAME GOALS, WORKING TOGETHER TO GIVE YOUR CHILD THE BEST POSSIBLE EDUCATION.

So, you see, even after your child enters school, the help you can give is not all over.

Both your child and his or her teacher depend on you for the kind of help only you can give, because

YOU WILL ALWAYS BE THE MOST IMPORTANT PERSON IN YOUR CHILD'S EDUCATION

A Final Word to Parents

Although this book ends here, the help you can give your children doesn't have to.

By helping your children be ready for school you have shown them that you value them, care what happens to them, and expect them to do well. By continuing to show that you care, you not only help your children to be 'ready to learn' *for the rest of their lives,* **but you are teaching them the most valuable lessons in the world; self-respect and respect for others. You are the best person to teach them these important lessons.**

Today, the world asks children to deal with many things that they have not had to deal with before. These lessons of confidence and concern will make it possible for your children to do their best with both the obstacles and opportunities their futures will present.

Now! *You can order The Kindergarten Survival Handbook*

➢ *on our website, at www. parent-education.com*
  (where credit cards are accepted)

➢ *or by mailing this form, with payment or Purchase Order number*
  to: Parent Education Resources
  752 18 St, Santa Monica CA 90402

****

Please send

____*copies of the Kindergarten Survival Handbook @ $14.95 ea.* $_____

___*copies of El Manual de Cómo Sobrevivir*
        el Jardín de Niños   @$14.95 ea. $_____

                                           Subtotal $_____

Special discounts are available for large quantity orders
and non-profit agencies. Please telephone 310-458-9758
for our current discount schedule.

                                           Discount $_____

California addresses add 8.5% sales tax   *Tax* $_____

Orders for one to three books, add $3.95 shipping.
  Larger orders will be billed for UPS charges.   *Shipping* $_____

                                           TOTAL $_____

NAME_____DATE_____

ADDRESS_____

CITY_____STATE_____ZIP_____

PHONE_____FAX_____

E-MAIL_____

PAYMENT: Check_____ Money order_____Purchase Order #_____

<u>School or Agency orders</u>
Please be sure to include P.O. number, quantity of each book (English or Spanish) being ordered, the name and contact phone number of school or agency and purchasing agent, and both billing and shipping addresses.

<u>Shipping</u>
Please allow two weeks for delivery. Let us know if you have any time constraints and we will do our best to help you. Shipping costs will be added to your invoice.

<u>Satisfaction is Guaranteed!</u>   If the Handbook is not what you need, return it in good condition within 30 days for a full and prompt refund of your purchase price.

<u>Contact Us:</u> by phone or fax at 310-458-9758, or *<u>info@parent-education.com.</u>*

Also available from **Parent Education Resources...**
Workshops and Seminars for Parents, Teachers, & Administrative Personnel

Surviving and Thriving in Kindergarten and Beyond

For parents, child-care providers, and Nursery School staff in your community.

Parents and others who care for young children sometimes do not realize that they are children's first and most important teachers. This workshop helps parents and all who work with young children learn 1) how important they are in preparing children for a successful kindergarten experience, 2) what children need to know to be ready to go to school, 3) how to transform children's everyday world into an exciting learning environment, and 4) how to stay positively involved in children's education throughout the school years.

Everything You Need to Know to Work with Parents, But Nobody Told You...

For Teachers, Teacher's Aides, Parent Involvement Specialists, and others who work with the parents of school-age children.

More and more, teachers are being asked to work with parents to involve them in their children's education. But working with parents requires skills and insights different from those needed to work with children, and teachers often need special tools and training to do this. This workshop explores some of the most important issues teachers need to consider when working to enlist parents as effective teachers of their children and as partners in their education.

The Parent Partnership Training Model

For Administrative personnel: A systematic strategy for successful, individualized home-school partnerships.

Successful plans for home-school partnerships must take into account the unique characteristics of the people and circumstances in the communities for which they are designed. This is especially true when the school community includes heterogeneous, ethnically diverse, or hard-to-reach-populations. The PPPM provides an overall framework which permits educators to design, implement, and evaluate their own, individualized strategies for developing effective home-school partnerships.

Migrant Families and School Readiness

For teachers and all those who work with migrant families and their children.

Helping migrant families prepare their children to succeed in school requires an understanding of their special strengths as well as the many obstacles with which they contend. This workshop explores ways by which those who work with migrant families can help them recognize and draw upon these strengths and become effective teachers of their own children.

Bridging the Gap: Reaching out to Parents of Diversity

For teachers and all school personnel.

The increasing ethnic and cultural diversity of America's school children presents a new and special challenge to teachers throughout the country. This workshop helps teachers and all school personnel bridge the gap between the perspectives and expectations of parents from a variety of cultures and their own, in order to work together comfortably and effectively, and help parents become important contributors to their children's success in America's schools.

For additional information about these seminars, please contact **Parent Education Resources**
752 18th St., Santa Monica, CA 90402 ☎ / FAX (310) 458-9758